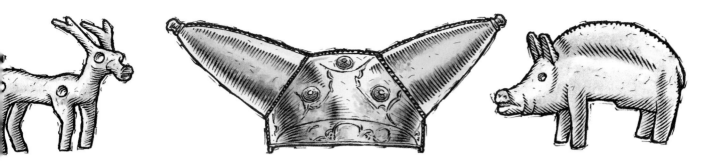

FLASHBACK HISTORY

CELTS

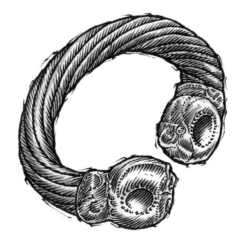

Dereen Taylor

PowerKiDS
press

New York

Published in 2010 by The Rosen Publishing Group Inc.
29 East 21st Street, New York, NY 10010

First Edition

Library of Congress Cataloging-in-Publication Data

Taylor, Dereen.
  Celts / Dereen Taylor.
     p. cm. — (Flashback history)
  Includes index.
  ISBN 978-1-4358-5516-8 (library binding)
  ISBN 978-1-4358-5517-5 (paperback)
  ISBN 978-1-4358-5518-2 (6-pack)
  1. Celts—Juvenile literature. I. Title.
  D70.T39 2010
  936.4—dc22

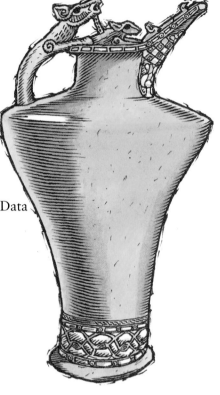

2009001861

Picture Acknowledgements: Front Cover; Magnum/Eirch Lessing; Ancient Art & Architecture Collection,
33b; Ashmolean Museum, Oxford, 15b; Bernisches Historiches Museum, Bern, Switzerland, 15t, 25b;
Bompiani Editore, 35t; British Library, 37b; British Museum, 8t, 12r, 13t, 14, 19b, 22, 23l, 24t, 27t, 28,
30, 32, 35b, 41l, 41r; C.M. Dixon, 16; English Heritage Photo Library, 17l, 33t, 42; Robert Harding
Picture Library/Michael Jenner, 18t, 29b; Michael Holford, 43t, Irish Tourist Board, 43b; Magnum/Erich
Lessing, 9, 13b, 17r, 19t, 20, 20r, 25t; Manchester Museum, 21; Musée Calvet Avignon, 37t, 40;
Nationalmuseet, Copenhagen, endpapers, 26; National Museum of Ireland, 39l; National Museums
of Scotland, 27b; Scala, 8b; Staatliche Museeu Preußisher, Kulturbesitz, Berlin, 34 (Ingrid Geske); The
Board of Trinity College, Dublin, 36; Unichrome (Bath) Ltd, 29t; Werner Forman Archive, 12l, 18b,
23r, 39r; Wuttembergisches Landesmuseum, Stuttgart, 30, 31, 38, 39

Endpapers: This silver panel is part of a cauldron that was found at Gundestrop in Denmark.

Manufactured in China

CONTENTS

Words that appear in **bold** can be found in the glossary on page 44.

WHO WERE THE CELTS?

The Celts lived in parts of Europe from the eighth century BCE to the middle
of the first century CE. They came from Hallstatt in
Austria. If you look at the map on page 9, you will
see how they moved from Hallstatt to other parts
of Europe. They traveled to northern Italy, Spain,
France, and Britain.

▶ METALWORKERS

Before the time of the Celts, bronze was the metal used
in Europe for making tools and weapons. Then the Celts
found a way to turn **iron ore** into metal. Since there was
lots of iron ore, they could make more metal tools, such
as this dagger and sheath.

▼ A STATUE OF A CELT

There are many clues that tell us what the Celts looked like.
We can look at the pictures made on tools and weapons by
Celtic craftspeoples. We can read about the Celts in books
written by the Romans. This statue
of a Celt is in Rome.
It celebrates one
of the Roman
victories over
the Celts.

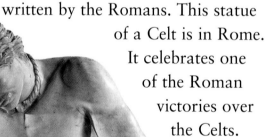

◀ HALLSTATT AND LA TENE

There are two Celtic periods. The first is from 750 to 450 BCE. It is called Hallstatt, after the area where the Celts were first known. The second period is from 450 BCE to 50 CE. It is called La Tene after a settlement in Switzerland. This picture shows that La Tene is now under water. In Celtic times, it was on dry land.

▼ THE CELTIC WORLD

The Celts were good farmers who grew lots of food. As the number of Celts increased, they spread out across Europe. They were looking for more land to farm. Some Celts became **mercenary** soldiers in other countries' armies. The different groups of Celts were never ruled by one leader. They were separate **tribes,** such as those shown on this map of Britain.

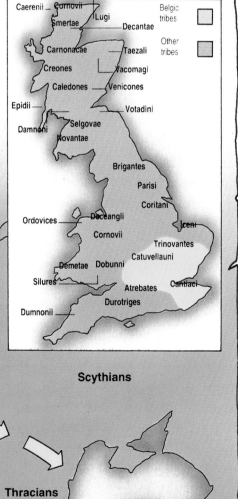

Hallstatt Culture
7th–5th Centuries BCE

La Tene Culture
(additional to
Hallstatt area)

Earliest La Tene

Earliest Hallstatt

La Tene raids and
influence

Ierne

Britain

Germans

Scythians

Gaul

Hallstatt

La Tene

Pannonia

Dacians

Thracians

Celtiberia

Etruria

Sabines

Iberia

Magna
Graeca

Galatians

TIMELINE	BCE 800–500	500–300	300–250	250–200	200–100
IN CENTRAL EUROPE	The earliest known Celtic **civilization** started at Hallstatt in Austria from around 750.	The Celtic civilization La Tene starts on the shores of Lake Neuchâtel in Switzerland from 500 onward.	In the east, Celts start to settle in Moravia around 300.	In 218, local Celtic **tribes** help to guide Hannibal's army through the Alps. About half of Hannibal's army is made up of Celts.	
IN WESTERN EUROPE	By the sixth century, there are Celtic settlements in France, Spain, Belgium, and the British Isles.				In 198, the Romans set out to conquer Gaul.

Bronze plaque

Romulus and Remus

| **IN SOUTHERN EUROPE** | Rome is said to be founded by Romulus in 753. Celts settle in northern Italy in the sixth century. | In Italy, the Celts defeat the Etruscans around 474. Between 390 and 387, the Celts defeat the Roman army. They fail to capture Rome. | Around 300, the Celts join the Etruscans to fight against the growth of the Roman Empire. | In 225, the Celts are defeated by the Romans at the battle of Telamon. | The Romans take control of Spain in 197. From 190, the Celts fight against Roman rule in Spain. |
| **EVENTS AROUND THE WORLD** | In 521, Darius becomes ruler of the Persian Empire. | Carthage controls the Mediterranean from North Africa. | In 278, 20,000 Celts move to Asia Minor to fight against the Syrians. 4,000 Celts go to Egypt to fight with Ptolemy II in 277. | In 237, Carthage conquers Celtic territory in Spain. Rome defeats the Carthaginians in Spain, in 206. | In 146, the Romans conquer North Africa and Greece. |

Persian carving

100–50	50–0	0–100 CE	100–400	400–
In 60, 32,000 Celts leave Bohemia to join the Helvetii Celts in Austria and Switzerland.		By 74, Romans have taken over all Celtic land in Central Europe.	The Age of Migrations starts. People from Asia and Eastern Europe start to move westward.	The Age of Migrations continues.
In 58, Julius Caesar begins to conquer Gaul. Between 55 and 54, he invades Britain. He later withdraws.	From 50, more of the Belgae Celts settle in southern Britain.	Claudius orders the invasion of Britain in 43.	In 122, the Romans build Hadrian's Wall. It stretches from the river Tyne to the Solway. It separates Celtic Britain to the north from Roman Britain to the south.	The Roman army leave Britain in the fifth century. Celtic civilization continues in Ireland, Scotland, Wales, and Cornwall.
In 93, the Romans finally defeat the Celtic uprisings in Spain.	Fighting against Roman rule in Gaul continues.		In 284, the Roman Empire is split and ruled from two capital cities. These are Rome and Constantinople.	German armies from the north throw out the last Roman Emperor in 476.
			In 220, the Han dynasty falls in China. In 320, the Gupta Empire is Founded in India.	

Dying Gaul statue

Bronze axe

Gold coin

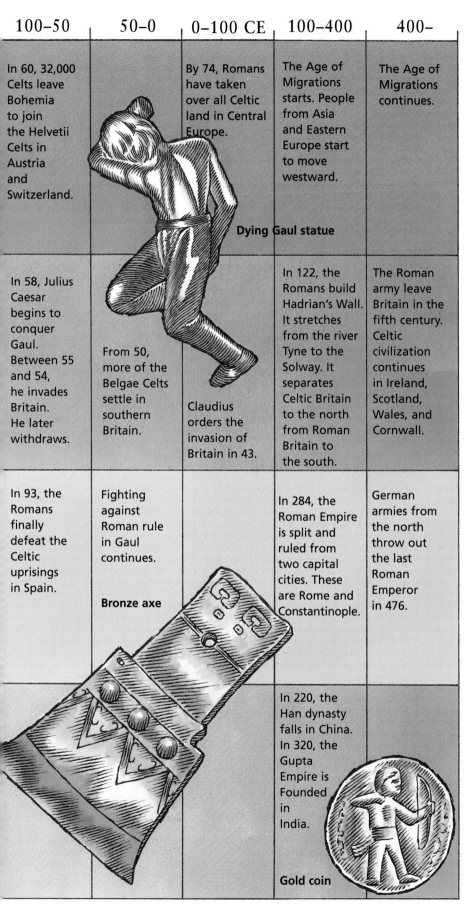

THE CELTS AS OTHERS SAW THEM

The Celts never wrote about themselves. But other people wrote about what they were like. The Greek historian, Diodorus Siculus, said the Celts were tall and had blond hair. He also said that Celtic noblemen shaved their cheeks, but let their moustaches grow over their mouths. Julius Caesar (100–44 BCE) said the Celts liked war and were always ready to go to battle. But they soon gave up the fight if the battle was being lost. Caesar also said the Celts made human **sacrifices** to their own gods.

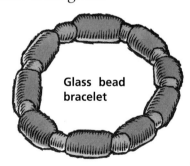

Glass bead bracelet

We must remember that the people who wrote about the Celts thought their way of life was better than the Celtic way of life.

DID THE CELTS GROW THEIR OWN FOOD?

Most Celts were farmers. They used their iron axes to clear the forests, which covered large parts of Europe at that time. The land was then used for growing crops such as rye, wheat, barley, and beans. The barley was used for making flour and also beer. Cattle were kept for meat and milk. Sheep were kept for meat as well as for their wool. The wool was spun and woven into cloth.

▼ CELTIC FIELDS

Celtic fields were usually square or oblong. They could be plowed in one day with a plow pulled by two oxen. This photograph shows a **reconstruction** of a Celtic farm in Hampshire, England.

Shears

Scythe

▲ FARMING TOOLS

By 500 BCE, Celtic farming tools were similar to the ones still being used at the start of the twentieth century. The scythe shown here was attached to a wooden handle and used to cut hay. The shears were used to clip wool from sheep in the summer.

▶ STORING GRAIN

Grain that had been harvested was stored in pits. The pits were about 6 feet (1.8 m) deep and lined with **wicker** or stone.

◀ LOOKING AFTER STOCK

In Celtic times, wolves and bears still lived in most parts of Europe. Farmers fired iron-tipped arrows like these at wild animals that attacked their cattle and sheep.

FARMING

The Roman general Julius Caesar visited Britain in 55 BCE. He found there were many farms and many cattle there. He said that the people who lived inland did not grow grain, but lived on milk and meat instead.

▶ HUNTING

Hunting was important to the Celts. They usually hunted on horseback and used spears to kill the animals. This bronze model from Spain shows they hunted the wild boar that lived in the forests.

DID THE CELTS GO SHOPPING?

The Celts did not go shopping like we do. Instead, they grew their own food and made most of the things they needed. But special things, like jewelry, was bought from craftspeople. Many craftspeople traveled around selling their wares.

▼ A BRONZE MIRROR

Roman writers said that the Celts were proud of how they looked. The men washed their hair with lime water to make it stand up in stiff tufts. This decorated mirror belonged to a woman, but it is likely men would have also bought mirrors to see how they looked.

▼ MAKING A TORQUE

A Celt would buy a gold **torque** rather than make one himself. This one was made from gold wire. Eight fine strands were twisted into a thicker strand (1). When eight of these were made, they were twisted together (2). Decorations were put on the ends to finish the torque (3).

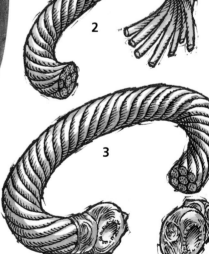

◄ GLASS BRACELETS

By 250 BCE, some Celts in southern and central Europe were making bracelets out of glass. As you can see from this photograph, they knew how to make different-colored glass. They did this by adding small amounts of copper and iron to the glass when it was in a liquid form. Many of the glassmakers sold the things they made from workshops in trading centers.

⚙ CELTIC TOWNS ⬡

As the number of Celts grew, some of them settled in groups called oppida. These were large villages often built on the tops of hills. Many of the people who lived in the oppida were farmers. Others made a living by producing goods like the ones shown here. Local farmers from surrounding areas brought their extra food to the oppida. They would sell or **barter** it for other goods.

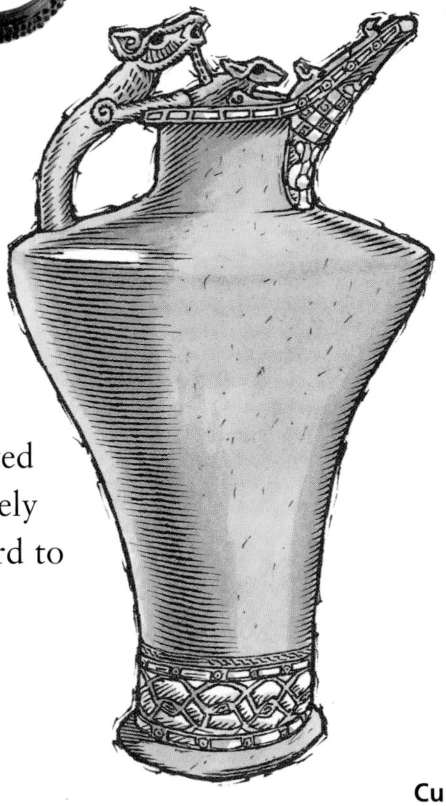

▶ A BRONZE JUG

The Celts used simple jugs made from plain pottery. But for special occasions, they might have used something like this grand wine jug. It is made from bronze and decorated with coral and **enamel**. It is likely only very rich Celts could afford to buy something like this.

▶ CURRENCY BARS

Iron bars have been found at many Celtic sites. The bars could have been exchanged for goods before coins came into use. They could also be given to a traveling craftspeople. He would melt them down and use them to repair tools.

Currency bars

DID THE CELTS HAVE FAMILIES LIKE OURS?

We do not know much about the structure of early Celtic families. From later times in Ireland, we know that a family was made up of the four generations who all came from the same great-grandfather. The land belonged to the whole group. The head of the family was usually a male relative.

▲ MEN AND WOMEN

This bronze head shows a Celtic man wearing a **torque** around his neck. The torque shows how important he was. It tells us that he was probably a warrior, as well as a farmer and the head of his family.

A man was usually the head of the family, but it seems many women were treated as equals. In some noble families, women became rulers. Many of them were buried with their valuable jewelry.

► CHILDREN

This plaque shows a girl combing a goddess's hair. It is a rare image of a Celtic child. Children didn't go to school and probably had to help their parents as soon as they could be useful and were old enough.

FAMILY PETS ▼

This bronze model of a dog was found in England. Many little models of dogs have been found. It is likely that dogs were kept as family pets, as well as being working dogs.

THE OLD AND THE POOR

The Celts looked after people who were old, poor, or sick. They gave them clothes, food, and shelter. As early as 300 BCE, the Celtic **tribes** in Ireland ran hospitals.

WOMEN'S WORK ►

Celtic women prepared all the food for their families. Another task was making woolen cloth. After the sheep had been clipped, the knots were combed out of the fleece with combs like these made from bone. The fleece was then spun into yarn on a spindle. Wool combs have been found on many Celtic sites.

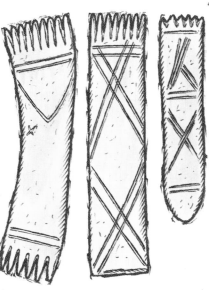

Wool combs

DID THE CELTS LIVE IN HOUSES?

No complete houses from Celtic times still exist. But **archaeologists** have found enough remains to know what Celtic houses looked like. They know that many of the houses were round, and the walls were usually built of stone. The roofs were thatched with straw or reeds.

▶ DUN CARLOWAY BROCH

Some of the Celts in Scotland lived in stone towers called brochs. These were round and had a double wall with a stone staircase running up inside it.

▼ THE HOUSE AT LITTLE BUSTER

This is a **reconstruction** of a Celtic house. Its framework is made from tree trunks. The roof is thatched with straw. The walls are made from a mixture of twigs and mud, called wattle and daub. The way into the house is through a wooden door.

INSIDE A CELTIC HOUSE ▶

As this photograph shows, a Celtic house had just one big room. The fire burning in the middle gave heat and light. It was also used for cooking. There was no chimney and sparks from the fire could set the thatched roof on fire.

Wine jug

Wine jug

Large dish

Cauldron and chain

FURNITURE

Archaeologists have found the remains of very little Celtic furniture. At night, people slept on the floor wrapped up in the skins of bears and wolves to keep warm.

▼ COOKING

The Celts cooked over an open fire. They used pans with round bottoms like this cauldron.

▲ EATING A MEAL

The Celts sat on the floor to eat. Food was served in dishes made of wood or pottery. There were knives but not forks. Some food would be eaten using fingers. Wine and beer would be drunk with a meal.

WHO WENT TO WORK IN THE CELTIC LANDS?

Most Celts worked for themselves on their own farms. Women and children helped with the work. Some Celts probably had slaves to help them, since slave chains have been found. Metalworkers and smiths made the things people could not make themselves. These included tools, weapons, and jewelry.

▼ SCRIBES

This **reconstruction** shows a Celtic smith's forge. The smith heated a bar of iron in the fire until it was red hot. Then he put it on the **anvil** to hammer it into the shape he wanted.

▶ MINING SALT

At Hallstatt, salt miners dug into the mountainside and then dug tunnels into the salt with picks. Torches like these helped them to see in places where there was no daylight.

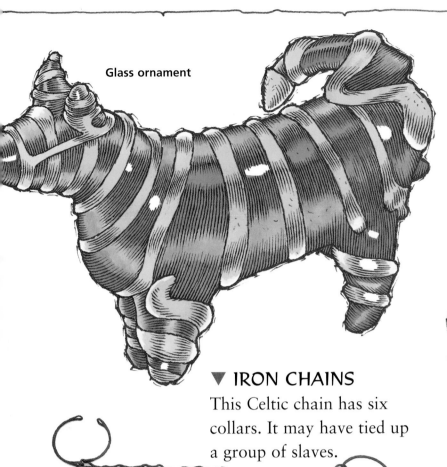

Glass ornament

◀ GLASSWORKERS

Glassworkers could only make a small amount of glass at a time. It was used for beads, bracelets, and ornaments like this little dog.

Bucket

▼ IRON CHAINS

This Celtic chain has six collars. It may have tied up a group of slaves.

▲ BRONZEWORKERS

Buckets and bowls were usually made of wood. For special occasions, the wood was covered with thin sheets of bronze. The handle was also made of bronze.

SLAVES

We think slaves were important to the Celts in two different ways. First, they helped with work around the farms. Second, the Celts could exchange slaves for other goods that they wanted. This slave trade was very important as the

Roman Empire grew. The Romans used slave labor to run the mines and farms that supported the Empire. Some of these slaves were Celts who had been defeated by Romans. Others had been sold into slavery. They were often exchanged for wine.

WHO DID THE CELTS TRADE WITH?

The Celtic **civilization** lasted a long time and covered a wide area. This meant the Celts traded with people from many different countries. The earliest trade was in salt from the mines around Hallstatt. Then weapons, pottery, slaves, and wine were traded among the tribes of Celts and also with people from other countries. Trade between the Celts and the Romans probably helped the Roman Empire to grow.

► LUXURY GOODS

This silver cup comes from the first century BCE. It was probably made in Italy, but it was found in a **chieftain's tomb** in England in 1906. Rich Celts in Britain had bronze, glass objects, and statues. These came from Rome before the Roman Conquest.

Roman pottery also came to Britain at this time. Some of it was good quality, but a lot of it was a cheap copy of the original pottery. Later, potters in southern Britain made their own copies of Roman pottery. These were traded as far north as Scotland.

► ENAMEL WARE

Skilled craftspeoples knew how to decorate their products with **enamel**. The most popular color was red, but they also used blue and yellow. Enamel was used on some shields and helmets. This decorated bronze plaque is part of a horse's harness. It was found in France in the first or second century BCE. It was probably made in Britain.

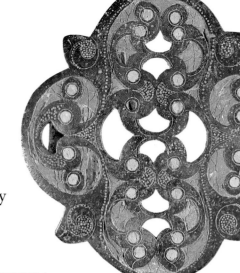

◄ ROMAN POTTERY

This photograph shows **grave goods**. They were found in the tomb of a Celtic chieftain in Britain. The four large pots in the background came from Rome. They were filled with wine and fish sauce from Spain.

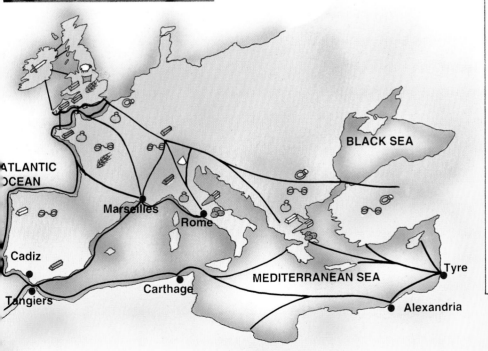

▼ TRADE ROUTES

As this map shows, the Celts traded goods across most of Europe and around the Mediterranean. Celtic traders transported goods by land and by sea.

KEY

⚔	Weapons
🐑	Wool
	Hides
	Tin
	Lead
	Bronzeware
	Silverware
	Gold
	Slaves
	Craft goods
	Wine
	Pottery
	Grain
	Salt
	Oil

ATLANTIC OCEAN

BLACK SEA

Marseilles

Rome

Cadiz

Tangiers

Carthage

MEDITERRANEAN SEA

Tyre

Alexandria

WHAT DID THE CELTS WEAR?

Celtic clothes needed to be hard-wearing. Men wore woolen trousers and a sleeveless shirt fastened with brooches. In the winter, men wore a cloak, women wore a long-skirted gown and a shawl. The Celts liked bright colors and material patterned with squares and stripes.

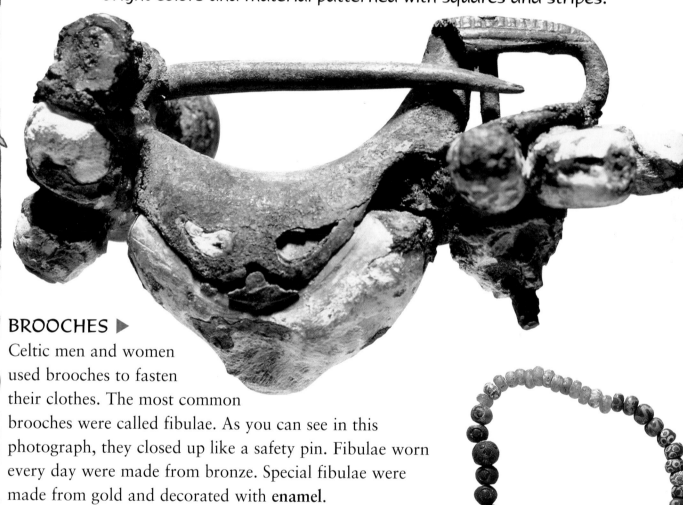

BROOCHES ▶

Celtic men and women used brooches to fasten their clothes. The most common brooches were called fibulae. As you can see in this photograph, they closed up like a safety pin. Fibulae worn every day were made from bronze. Special fibulae were made from gold and decorated with **enamel**.

JEWELRY ▶

Many Celtic women wore glass beads around their necks. Often the beads were plain, but blue beads with a white pattern were also very popular. Finger and toe rings, and bronze and gold bracelets, were worn by some women.

FOOTWEAR ▶

This workman's shoe was found in the salt mines at Hallstatt. The salt stopped the leather from rotting. Most Celts probably wore shoes like these. But some shoes trimmed with gold have also been found.

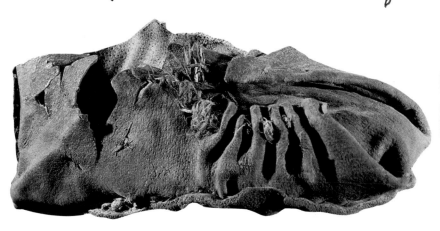

▼ MAKING CLOTHES

The woman below probably made all the clothes that her family needed. First she spun wool into yarn. Then she colored the yarn with vegetable dyes. She could then weave it into patterned cloth on a loom. She cut the clothes from the cloth and sewed them together with a needle made from bone.

Bronze belt

🪲 HOW WE KNOW 🦋

Cloth soon rots in the ground. This is why no complete pieces of Celtic clothing have ever been found. Brooches have been found with bits of dull brown cloth still pinned to them. When **archaeologists** study the cloth, they can find out what dyes were used to color the yarn. The dyes came from plants like woad, madder, and weld. These made the colors blue, red, and yellow.

▲ A BRONZE BELT

Celtic women usually wore long, loose gowns. They used cloth or leather belts to pull their gowns in at the waist. Only wealthy women had belts made from bronze, like this one from Sweden.

WHAT DID THE CELTS DO IN THEIR SPARE TIME?

Celtic farmers had to look after their crops and animals all year round. But they still found time to enjoy sports and games. They also celebrated religious festivals each year. Two of these were Samhain on November 1 and Beltane on May 1. Celebrations included feasting, drinking, and music.

CELTIC FEASTS ▲

There was lots of drinking at Celtic feasts. Most people drank beer, which they made from barley. Wealthy Celts probably drank wine. The wine was served in bowls like this silver cauldron from Denmark.

The Celts ate plenty of pork and **venison** at their feasts. The meat was roasted on a spit over the fire. When it was cooked, it was divided up so that the most important people got to eat the best parts.

PLAYING GAMES ▶

Playing pieces have been found in Celtic sites and graves. The pieces in this photograph are part of a set of 24. They are made of glass and can be divided by color into four groups.

Trumpet

◀ MUSIC AND DANCING

There are written descriptions of the Celts enjoying music and dancing. But only a few musical instruments have ever been found.

Carnyx

SAMHAIN AND HALLOWEEN

Samhain was the name of the Celtic New Year. It was celebrated on November 1, which was the start of winter. The farm animals were brought together. Some were kept and some were killed for food. Samhain was thought to be a time of magic. People were able to pass into the world of spirits and then return. The memory of some of this magic is now celebrated on October 31 as Halloween.

HORSE RIDING ▶

Horses were a means of transportation. But it is likely the Celts also rode for pleasure. This pony cap was found in Scotland. The holes are for the pony's ears to stick out of. The horns were added to the cap later.

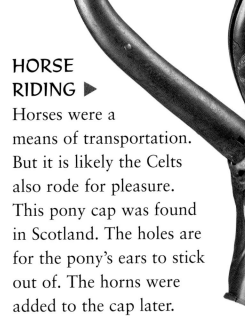

WHO DID THE CELTS WORSHIP?

The Celts had many different gods and goddesses. Nature was an important part of their religion. Many gods were linked to streams and trees. The Celtic **tribes** in Britain had religious leaders called Druids. They were like wise men or witch doctors who demanded **sacrifices**.

◀ THE EARLY GODS

An early Celtic goddess is Epona. She was the horse goddess. She was sometimes shown as a horse's head, as in this photograph. Epona was the goddess of fertility. Sacrifices to her would help the crops to grow.

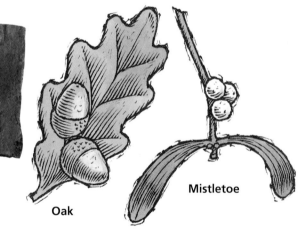

Mistletoe

Oak

▲ SACRED GROVES

We know the Celts had some temples. But many of their religious activities took place in **sacred** groves hidden among the trees. The Druids looked after these groves. Ordinary people were not allowed to go too close to them. The most sacred tree was the oak. Mistletoe was also sacred and could only be cut by a Druid with a gold sickle.

◀ ROMAN AND CELTIC GODS

When the Romans invaded Britain in 43 CE, they built temples to their own gods. These included Mercury, Mars, and Neptune. But they also included the old Celtic gods in the names of some of the towns they built. They gave the name Aquae Sulis to the city we now call Bath. Sulis was a Celtic goddess. The Roman name meant "waters of Sulis." This carving from Bath shows a Roman image of a Celtic god.

▼ CHRISTIAN CELTS

The Celts in Britain became Christians in late Roman times. They carved crosses like this one in Ireland, built in the tenth century CE.

▼ HEALING

The Celts often made sacrifices to the gods if they were sick. They also used herbs and medicines to treat their illnesses. Surgeons did operations using instruments like these.

◉ THE DRUIDS ✝

The Druids were religious leaders. They were political leaders, too, and might decide whether to go to war with another tribe. Druids studied for many years to perform religious ceremonies. The Druids sometimes asked for sacrifices.

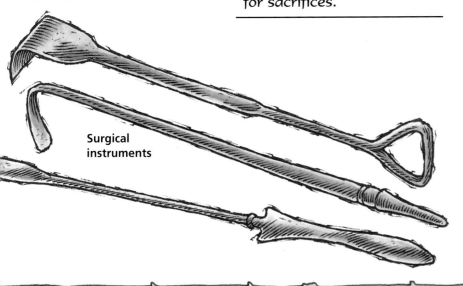

Surgical instruments

DID THE CELTS BELIEVE IN LIFE AFTER DEATH?

The Celts believed life continued after death. The dead moved on to another world, known as the Otherworld. Life continued in the Otherworld, but people could also die there, too. When this happened, the person was reborn back in this world. The Celts usually buried their dead with things that would be useful in their next life. These included clothes and food.

◀ BURIALS

This photograph shows a Celtic grave that has been dug up in Britain. It is known as a chariot or a cart burial. This is because a chariot was placed in the grave with the body. The body was usually put on its side in a crouching position. In some chariot graves, the bones of horses have also been found. But it seems the Celts only used worn-out chariots and old horses for these burials. Most bodies in chariot graves have been buried with jewelry and weapons, such as a sword and spearheads.

▼ A COUCH FROM A PRINCELY TOMB

The graves of rich Celts are often known as princely **tombs**. This bronze couch was inside a tomb found in Germany. A body had been laid on the couch. There was also a cart, a cauldron, nine drinking horns, and nine plates inside the tomb.

FOOD AND DRINKS ▶

It is common to find things to do with eating and drinking in Celtic tombs. Some people have been buried with meat and even cauldrons to cook the meat in. Pottery cups, plates, and pots have been found. **Archaeologists** can study the pottery to find out what it is made of and where it was made.

Pottery containers

Drinking horn

▲ GRAVE ROBBERS

Grave robbers have stolen many of the precious objects the Celts buried with their dead. This gold drinking horn is one of a pair missed by robbers. It was found by archaeologists in Germany.

CELTIC FUNERALS

The Celts were said to cry at a birth and laugh at a funeral. They thought that the dead person went to the Otherworld and that everyone would meet there again. From the first century BCE, many bodies were burned or cremated. The remains of their bones were placed in pots. These were sometimes buried with **grave goods** to help the person on their way to the next life. When the Celts became Christians, they stopped burying grave goods with their dead.

WHO RULED THE CELTS?

The Celts were never ruled as a single empire. Instead, each **tribe** had its own leader. The leader was from the noble or warrior class. Apart from nobles and warriors, Celts were split into farmers and learned men. Doctors, Druids, poets, and metalworkers were all learned men.

THE SNETTISHAM TORQUE

Warriors wore **torques**, like this one from Snettisham in Norfolk. They were usually made of gold or a mixture of gold and silver called electrum. Torques were very valuable.

Gold coins

GOLD COINS ▶

By the second century BCE, the Celts were using coins. The Coins were mostly made from gold. Each tribe had its own coins. The name of the tribe's ruler was usually on the coins.

◀ HILL FORTS

This is a view from the sky of Maiden Castle in Dorset, England. The ditches around this hill fort protected the Celts from their enemies. The houses were built in the open area on top of the hill.

FRIENDS AND FOES

As the Roman Empire grew, some Celtic tribes joined together to fight against the Roman soldiers. But some Celts welcomed the new rulers. This led to Celts fighting against Celts. In 43 CE, King Caratacus was defeated when he tried to fight the Romans. He fled to the northern British queen, Carimandua. She betrayed Caratacus to the Romans.

Warrior
god statue

▼ QUEEN OF THE ICENI

This statue shows the Celtic queen Boudicca or Boadicea. She ruled the Iceni tribe in eastern England after her husband's death in 60 CE. She led her people against the rule of the Romans. The Romans eventually defeated the Iceni.

▲ GODS

Warriors were very important in Celtic society. This bronze statue from France shows a warrior-god from the second century BCE.

WERE THERE ANY CELTIC ARTISTS?

Early Celts did not paint pictures. Instead, their artists decorated pots and weapons. They used gold, silver, and bronze to make beautiful patterns and made bronze figures of dogs and wild boars. Some artists put **enamel** patterns on metal. Later, Celts carved patterns on memorial stones. We still use some Celtic patterns today.

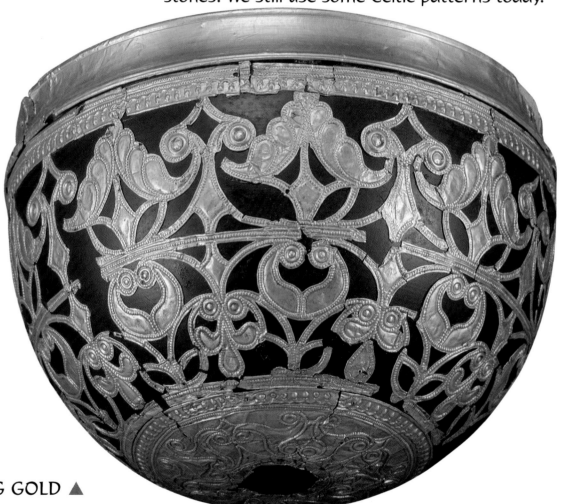

USING GOLD ▲

This wooden cup was made in the fifth century BCE. It has been decorated with thin sheets of gold, called gold leaf. Some of the gold has been raised to show the pattern more clearly. The cup was found in the **tomb** of a rich man in Germany. The wooden cup had rotted away, but the metalwork had survived. **Archaeologists** made a new cup to fit into the metalwork. Patterned strips of gold have also been found in tombs. They were used to decorate shoes.

AN ORNAMENTAL HELMET ▶

This iron helmet is from a **chieftain's** tomb in Romania. The bird on the top is made from bronze. The bird's wings move up and down as if it were flying. The helmet was worn for special occasions. It would not have been worn in battle. The bird would make it too easy to knock the helmet off the owner's head.

ENAMELING ▶

The Celts heated the enamel mixture until it melted (1). They roughened the part that they wished to decorate (2). This made sure that the enamel would stick when it was poured in (3).

FAVORITE PATTERNS

The Celts liked designs made from straight lines and swirling patterns. These looked like the stems and leaves of plants. Some popular animal designs included geese and hares. The Celts believed these animals were magical.

◀ MAKING CIRCLES

This bronze plaque has a pattern made from circles. The circles were made with iron compasses. One way to make a pattern was to make a wax model of the object and put the pattern on the model. The model was covered in clay and heated to melt the wax. Melted bronze was then poured into the mold and left to get hard.

DID THE CELTS WRITE BOOKS?

The Druids would not let the Celts read or write. But the Celts were still great story-tellers. Their poems, legends, and histories were passed down through families. They were written down when the power of the Druids ended. Later, Celts who became Christians made beautiful written copies of religious works.

◄ THE BOOK OF KELLS

This is a page from the Book of Kells. It is a handwritten copy of the Gospels from the Bible. It could take months or even years to make a book like this.

▼ CELTIC ALPHABETS

Celtic letters were made up of mostly straight lines so that they were easy to carve on stone. The alphabet below was used in Wales. The Ogham alphabet at the bottom of page 37 was used in Ireland and western Britain.

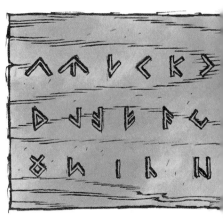

OTHER ALPHABETS

The Celts based their alphabets on the ones used by the people they met. This inscription from France is in a Celtic language. The letters are based on those used in Massilia, now Marseilles.

DATES AND CALENDARS

Calendars were one of the few things to be written down by the Druids. A calendar found in France was divided into sixteen columns. It had 62 months. The days were numbered and some days were labeled as good days for starting new activities.

KING ARTHUR ▶

The legend of King Arthur was first written down in the twelfth century CE. Arthur was born in Cornwall. He became king of Britain when he was 15. When he was wounded in battle, Arthur was taken to the Isle of Avalon. There his sword was thrown into the water as a sacrifice to the Lady of the Lake. This picture is from a fourteenth century telling of the story.

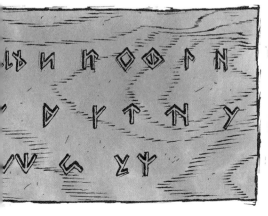

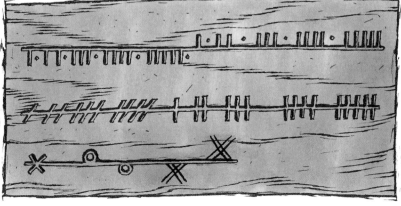

HOW DID THE CELTS TRAVEL?

The earliest Celts traveled on foot through the high mountain passes in the Alps. They carried everything they needed on their backs. On flatter ground, they traveled on horseback or in chariots and wagons. Many Celts lived by water, so they traveled in boats. Some Celts crossed the sea in small ships to trade with nearby countries.

A FOUR-WHEELED WAGON ▶

Celtic wagons and chariots were made mostly from wood. Because wood rots, no complete ones have survived. But **archaeologists** have found enough metal fittings and marks left in the soil to make the model wagon shown in this photograph. Two horses pulled this wagon.

They were attached to a wooden yoke at the end of the pole in the center.

MAKING A CHARIOT ▶

Chariots were often used in battle. A charioteer drove them. He had a warrior standing beside him. The warrior threw spears and also fought with his sword. The chariot was made in several parts. The wheels were made from wood and joined together (1). Then the body of the chariot and its pole were made and joined together (2). Then the sides were added (3). They protected the driver and his passenger.

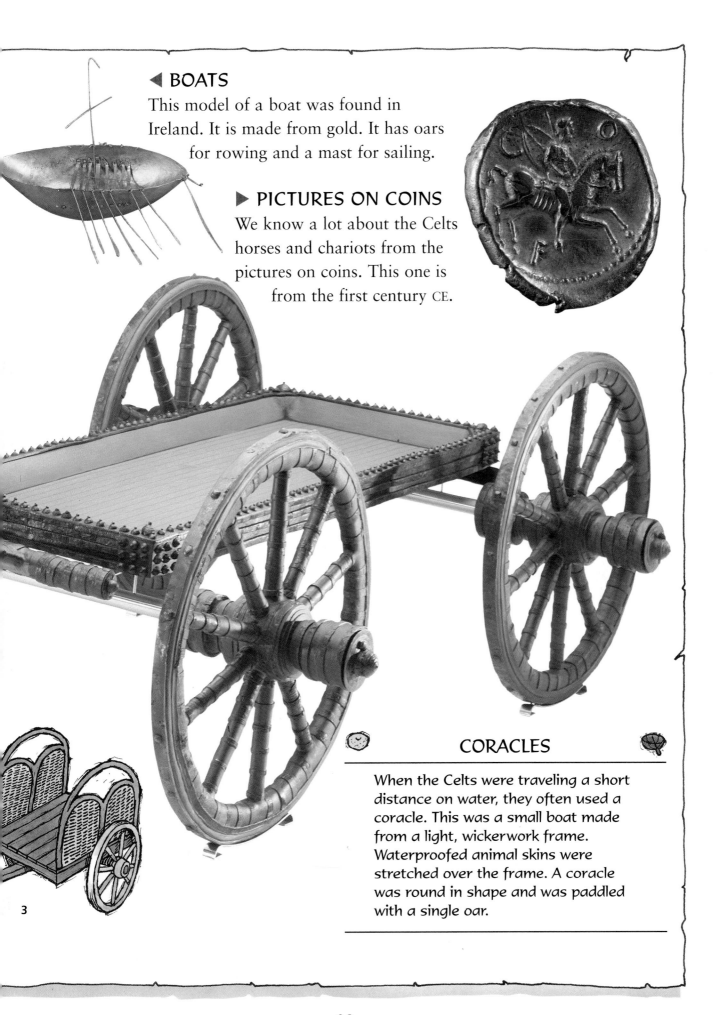

◀ BOATS
This model of a boat was found in Ireland. It is made from gold. It has oars for rowing and a mast for sailing.

▶ PICTURES ON COINS
We know a lot about the Celts horses and chariots from the pictures on coins. This one is from the first century CE.

CORACLES
When the Celts were traveling a short distance on water, they often used a coracle. This was a small boat made from a light, wickerwork frame. Waterproofed animal skins were stretched over the frame. A coracle was round in shape and was paddled with a single oar.

3

DID THE CELTS HAVE AN ARMY?

Celts were fierce warriors who loved fighting. They fought for their **tribe**, rather than their country. Celtic warriors fought on foot or in chariots. They did not often fight as an organized army. Instead, they used speed and fear to defeat their enemies. At first, the Celts were successful and won many battles. But eventually, the Roman army defeated them.

◀ A CELTIC WARRIOR

This is a statue of a Celtic warrior from Gaul. It is from the first century BCE. A tunic made from chain mail protects the warrior's body. His sword hangs from a belt. He carries a shield to protect himself. Celts were brave soldiers and often fought against much larger armies. If they were defeated in battle, many Celts killed themselves. This was because they did not want to be taken prisoner by the enemy.

WEAPONS ▶

A Celt's favorite weapon was his sword. It was usually very long and had a blade made from iron. It was used for slashing at the enemy soldier, rather than stabbing him. Other weapons included daggers, knives, and spears. The Celts also used battle-axes and bows and arrows. Another weapon was the slingshot. This was used to fire small, round stones.

Sword

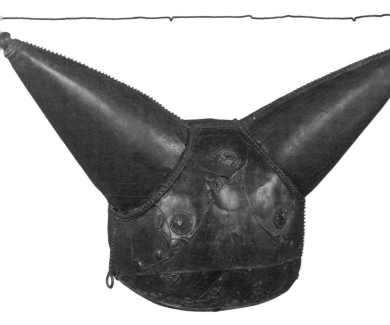

A HORNED HELMET ▲

This bronze helmet was found in the River Thames in London. It was made around the first century BCE. Soldiers probably only wore helmets like these for special occasions.

THE BATTERSEA SHIELD ▶

This shield was also found in the River Thames. It is made from wood, covered with bronze. The panels are decorated with **enamel**. Shields were usually made from wood or leather.

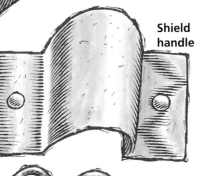

Shield handle

Rings to attach sword

CELTIC MERCENARIES

The Celts enjoyed fighting and were good at it. Many of them went to fight in other people's armies. They even fought for people who had been their enemies in the past. When Hannibal came from Carthage in 218 BCE, the Celts guided his army through the Alps. Around 10,000 Celtic warriors joined his army in Gaul to try and defeat the Romans there. When Hannibal had to return to Carthage, the Romans soon defeated the Celts.

WHAT HAPPENED TO THE CELTS?

As the Roman Empire increased, it took over most of the Celtic lands. The Celts began to live like the Romans. Some **tribes** accepted the Romans wanting to add Britain to their Empire. But others would not. In Scotland, Ireland, most of Wales, and Cornwall, the Celts managed to continue living their lives as they had before.

Irish settlement

Angles, Jutes, and Saxons

Irish advance

Anglian advance

▲ HADRIAN'S WALL

The Romans didn't conquer Scotland. They built Hadrian's Wall to protect the northern border of Britain. It was started in 122 CE and was 75 miles (120 km) long.

▶ AFTER THE ROMANS

The Roman soldiers left Britain at the start of the fifth century CE. **Angles, Jutes,** and **Saxons** soon invaded Britain from the east. They settled in the areas that had been ruled by the Romans. The Celts stayed in Scotland, Wales, and the southwest. They were joined by more Celts from Ireland.

◀ KING ARTHUR'S ROUND TABLE

In the Great Hall of the castle in Winchester is what is thought to be the Round Table. This is where King Arthur sat with his knights.

▼ LATE CELTIC JEWELRY

Celtic jewelry designs were copied for centuries. Brooches like this one were used to fasten cloaks. Queen Victoria wore one in the nineteenth century.

Brooch

THE CELTIC INHERITANCE

Many old Celtic tribes are remembered in place names. The Parisii gave their name to Paris. The Belgii gave their name to Belgium. Celtic languages are still used by people who speak Welsh, Gaelic, Erse, Manx, Cornish, and Breton.

▼ CELTIC CHRISTIANITY

After the Romans left Britain, Christianity died out in most places. But it continued to grow in Ireland. Monks built **monasteries** like this one at Ardmore. Many years later, monks from Ireland took Christianity back to Britain.

GLOSSARY, FURTHER INFORMATION, AND WEB SITES

ANGLES People from northern Germany who settled in eastern and northern England in the fifth century CE.

ANVIL A hard block on which a blacksmith hammers hot metal into shape.

ARCHAEOLOGIST A scientist who makes a study of the remains of the past.

BARTER To trade goods by exchanging them for other goods rather than for money.

BCE The abbreviation of "Before the common era," used to show that a date is before the present era, which started with the birth of Christ.

CE The abbreviation of "Christian era," used to show that a date is of the present era, which started with the birth of Christ.

CHIEFTAIN The leader of a tribe.

CIVILIZATION The cultural and social way of life developed by a nation of people.

ENAMEL A smooth, hard coating used to decorate metal.

GRAVE GOODS Special objects buried with a body. Celtic grave goods included jewelry, pottery, and sometimes horses.

IRON ORE Rocks from which the metal iron can be taken out.

JUTES People from northwest Germany who settled in southeast England in the fifth century CE.

MERCENARY Someone who fights for money or other rewards, rather than for himself or his leader.

MONASTERIES Places where religious men called monks live and work.

RECONSTRUCTION An object that has been made to look like the original.

SACRED Something of great religious importance.

SACRIFICES Valuable offerings made to please a god. Some sacrifices involved the killing of a person or an animal.

SAXONS People from west Germany who settled in southern England in the fifth century CE.

TOMBS A place where a dead person's body is buried. Some tombs are above the ground.

TORQUE A special collar, usually made of gold, worn by warriors around their necks.

TRIBES A group of families who live together and are ruled by a Chieftain.

VENISON Meat that comes from deer.

WICKER Slender twigs that can be woven together. They are usually taken from willow trees.

Books to read

Ancient Celts: Archaeology Unlocks the Secrets of the Celts' Past
by Jen Green (National Geographic Children's Books, 2008)

Life of the Ancient Celts
by Hazel Richardson (Crabtree Publishing, 2005)

People of the Ancient World: The Ancient Celts
by Patricia Calvert (Children's Press, 2005)

Web Sites

Due to the changing nature of Internet links, PowerKids Press has developed an online list of Web sites related to the subject of this book. This site is updated regularly. Please use this link to access this list:
www.powerkidslinks.com/flash/celts

INDEX

alphabets 36–7
animals 12, 13, 26, 27, 35
Arthur, King 37, 43
axes 11, 12, 40

beer 19, 26
Beltane 26
Boadicea, Queen 33
boats 38, 39
Book of Kells 36
bracelets 11, 15, 21, 24
brochs (towers) 18
bronze 8, 14, 15, 16, 17, 21, 22, 24, 31, 33, 34–5, 41
brooches 24, 25, 43
burials 30–1

Caesar, Julius 11, 13
calendars 37
Caratacus, King 33
Carimandua, Queen 33
cattle 12, 13
cauldrons 19, 26, 27, 31
chariots 30, 38, 39, 40
Christians 28, 29, 31, 36, 43
cloth 12, 17, 25
clothes 24–5, 30
coins 11, 15, 32, 39
cooking 19, 26
coracles 39
craftspeoples 8, 14–15, 23, 34–5
currency bars 15

Diodorus Siculus 11
Druids 28, 29, 32, 36–7
dyes 25

enamel 23, 24, 34, 35, 41

families 16–17
farming 9, 12–13, 15, 16, 20, 21, 26
feasts 26
festivals 26
food 9, 12–13, 19, 26, 30, 31
funerals 31
furniture 19

games 26, 27
glass 11, 15, 21, 22, 24, 27
gods and goddesses 17, 28–9, 33
gold 14, 24, 25, 28, 31, 32, 34, 39
grain pits 13
grave goods 23, 30–1
groves, sacred 28

Hadrian's Wall 11, 42
Hallstatt 8, 9, 10, 20, 22, 25
Hannibal 10, 41
helmets 35, 41
hill forts 33
hospitals 17
houses 18–19, 33
hunting 13

Iceni tribe 33
illnesses 29
iron 8, 12, 15, 20, 21, 40

jewelry 11, 14–15, 16, 20, 21, 24, 30, 43

La Tene 9, 10
languages 43
life after death 30–1

mercenary soldiers 9, 41
metalwork 8, 20, 32, 34–5
monasteries 43
music 26, 27

Otherworld 30, 31

place names 43
plows 12
pottery 15, 19, 22, 23, 31

religion 26, 28–9
Romans 8, 10–11, 21, 22, 23, 28, 29, 33, 40, 41, 42
rulers 32–3

sacrifices 11, 28, 29
salt 20, 22, 25
Samhain 26, 27
shields 40, 41
shoes 25, 34
silver 22, 26, 34
slaves 20, 21, 22
soldiers 9, 33, 40–1, 42
statues 8, 11, 22, 33, 40
swords 30, 38, 40–1

tombs 23, 31, 34
tools 8, 12, 20
torques 14, 16, 32
trade 21, 22–3
tribes 9, 32–3, 42

wagons 38–9
warriors 16, 32, 33, 38, 40
weapons 8, 20, 22, 30, 34, 38, 40–1
wine 19, 21, 22, 23, 26
women 16, 17, 20, 24–5, 33
wool 12, 17, 25